NORTHAMPTONSHIRE
AND THE
ABOLITION
OF
SLAVERY

KEY FIGURES, MOVEMENTS, AND MOMENTS

JACK PRESTON

ISBN: 9781068767173

First published in Great Britain by Kateringes Books, 2026

Part I - Setting the Scene: Slavery, Empire, and the Midlands

PART II - Movements, Churches, and Organisations

PART III — Northamptonshire's Key Figures

A Note on Language

In this book, you will sometimes see words that were used in the past to describe black people. One of these words is "negro." Today, this word is not respectful, and we do not use it in everyday language.

It appears here only when quoting old sources, where the word was written at the time. Keeping the original wording helps us understand history exactly as it was recorded.

Whenever the book is speaking in its own voice, it uses modern and respectful words.

Introduction:

The Monster is Dead

Full emancipation finally came into effect across the British Empire on 1 August 1838. The Baptist missionary William Knibb, born in Kettering and one of Northamptonshire's most powerful abolitionist voices, stood before a vast congregation in Jamaica and declared: **"The monster is dead."** [1]

All numbered references are listed from page 49.

"The monster" was the centuries-old system of slavery. To mark the monster's death, a coffin was buried containing manacles, a slave collar, and a whip.

But the monster didn't go down without a fight. The killing blow was *meant* to be when the British Parliament legislated the abolition of slavery in 1833.

But the beast clung on.

Thousands of formerly enslaved men and women were forced into a so-called "apprenticeship" system, which bound them to unpaid labour until 1838.

When that system was finally swept away, Knibb marked the moment with words that captured both triumph and exhaustion; the end of a long and bitter struggle.

Many of the weapons used to bring the monster down were made, or at least sharpened, in Northamptonshire.

Reforms which broadened who could vote were thanks to the county's own Lord Althorp, greatly amplifying the anti-slavery voice in Parliament.

And this was a voice which had already made itself heard. By the time of the voter Reform Acts, several waves of petitions had come from Northamptonshire, making the county's opinion loud and clear: the monster must die.

Some of these petitions were supported by a particularly powerful voice in the movement: the Baptist Church. Several pastors across the county were speaking up, and encouraging their congregations to do the same.

It was from a Baptist background that Knibb himself came, among many others in the movement.

The road to abolition was not smooth or straightforward, and it wasn't purely carried out by a handful of influential figures in Parliament. It was a movement built from thousands of acts of conscience; in chapels, meeting houses, parlours, and workshops, by people whose names are known and unknown.

Knibb's declaration was not simply a celebration. It was the summation of decades of protest, petitioning, preaching, and pressure by people across Britain, including here in Northamptonshire.

Their story is the story of how an idea took root in ordinary hearts and minds and became an unstoppable force for justice.

This book follows those ideas, those movements, and those people, showing how a county far from the Caribbean plantations became part of the great struggle to end one of history's gravest injustices.

PART I

Setting the Scene: Slavery, Empire, and the Midlands

What Was the Transatlantic Slave Trade?

From the early 1500s until the 1800s, millions of African men, women, and children were captured, sold, and transported across the Atlantic Ocean to work on plantations and in mines in the Caribbean, the Americas, and parts of South America.

European ships sailed in a three-part route commonly known as the 'Triangular Trade': manufactured goods from Europe to Africa; enslaved Africans to the Americas; and raw materials such as sugar, cotton, coffee, and tobacco back to Europe.

Conditions were horrific. People were chained together for weeks in cramped holds, living with disease, filth, and abuse. Mortality rates were high. Those who survived were sold into lifelong, hereditary slavery. They were forced to work under violent coercion for the profit of plantation owners, merchants, and industries.

Although Northamptonshire lay far from the sea, the county was not isolated from this global system. Local economies were quietly woven into the fabric of the Empire, and many Northamptonshire goods played supporting roles in the machinery that kept slavery operating …

Northamptonshire's Economic Links to the Slave Trade

Plantation-owning families

A number of Northamptonshire landowners held plantations in the Caribbean [4]. These families were part of the British absentee-owner class who lived comfortably in England while their incomes were generated by enslaved people thousands of miles away.

Shoemaking and leather

Northamptonshire has long been famous for its leatherwork and shoemaking. During the 1700s and early 1800s, large quantities of the county's leather goods were sold to the British Army and Royal Navy [2].

The Navy, in particular, was a central part of protecting and expanding Britain's empire, including escorting slave ships and maintaining the maritime routes they used.

Northamptonshire's craftsmen were not personally involved in the slave trade, but their products were part of the broader imperial supply chain.

Ironwork, tools, and hardware

The Midlands supplied the Atlantic world with iron which would have been used for goods such as shackles, nails, tools, and plantation equipment [3] . Not all of this originated in Northamptonshire, but the county was firmly embedded within the same regional manufacturing network.

Blacksmiths, ironmongers, and small industrial workshops contributed to an economy that benefited (directly or indirectly) from colonial demand.

Slave-ownership compensation (1830s)

When slavery was abolished in the British Empire in 1833, the government paid £20 million in compensation … not to formerly enslaved people, but to their *owners*.

The compensation records show that several Northamptonshire residents received payments for enslaved people they owned abroad [4].

Why Northamptonshire Matters

All of this local context is crucial. It shows that Northamptonshire was not a passive bystander, nor was it uniquely guilty: it was typical of many English counties whose everyday workforces, industries, and markets became entangled (often unknowingly) in the economic world built on enslaved labour.

It also explains why, when abolitionist ideas reached the county, they resonated so strongly and inspired so many people to demand change.

Although Northamptonshire never had ports, plantations, or slave-trading merchants on the grand scale of Bristol, London, or Liverpool, the county played a distinctive and revealing role in Britain's abolition story.

In many ways, Northamptonshire acts as a microcosm of the national debate, a place where religious conviction, political reform, and ordinary people's moral choices came together to push against one of the greatest injustices of the age.

A County of Dissent and Independent Thinking

For centuries, Northamptonshire was known for its strong tradition of Christian Nonconformity: Baptists, Independents, Quakers, and other dissenting groups flourished here, often in villages and small market towns rather than big urban centres.

These communities placed emphasis on personal conscience, Biblical equality, and the moral duty to challenge wrongdoing; all ideas that naturally aligned with early abolitionist thinking.

It was in Northamptonshire's chapels and meeting houses that sermons against cruelty were preached, petitions were organised, and parishioners were encouraged to think about the plight of the enslaved.

Ministers trained here, especially those connected to the Doddridge Academy and the Baptist networks, and carried these ideas across Britain and beyond.

Dissenters

In the eighteenth century, a Dissenter was any Christian who did not belong to the Church of England.

This included: Baptists; Independents (later called Congregationalists); Quakers; Presbyterians; and sometimes early Methodists

In Northamptonshire, the Dissenter tradition was especially strong, and many leading abolitionists came from Dissenter backgrounds.

Evangelicals

In the 1700s and early 1800s, Evangelical referred to any Christians (both inside and outside the Church of England) who emphasised:

- personal faith
- the authority of the Bible
- active, heartfelt religion
- moral responsibility
- spreading the Christian message at home and abroad.

Evangelicals were found among Anglicans, Baptists, Methodists, Independents, and other groups.

They were united not by a denomination but by a shared enthusiasm for practical action, including missionary work, social reform, and the abolition of slavery.

Ordinary County, Extraordinary Influence

What makes Northamptonshire stand out is not vast wealth or high-profile London connections; it is the way ordinary villages, chapels, and families became part of a nationwide moral struggle.

When Northamptonshire towns petitioned Parliament, they demonstrated that the call for abolition was not confined to ports or political elites. It was a movement rooted in everyday conscience.

In this sense, Northamptonshire's story exemplifies how the abolition of slavery was won: not by famous parliamentarians alone, but by thousands of people across counties like this one; thinking, debating, preaching, writing, and signing their names in the belief that slavery must end.

PART II

Movements, Churches, and Organisations

The Northamptonshire Anti-Slavery Petitions

If we want to see Northamptonshire's ordinary, un-named people in the abolition story, we have to look at the *petitions*. These were the documents, carried to Westminster in bundles, that turned private conviction into public pressure.

In the late 1780s and again in the 1830s, many of Northamptonshire's towns and parishes signed their names to calls for change.

The first great wave came in 1788, as the campaign to abolish the slave trade gathered momentum. The Northampton Mercury urged its readers to support a county petition "for the suppression of [a trade] replete with every species of oppression and cruelty." [5]

Shortly afterwards, a meeting of leading figures from across the county gathered at the George Inn in Northampton, under the chairmanship of Earl Spencer [6]. They agreed unanimously to petition the House of Commons for abolition of the trade.

To ensure this was not just the voice of one town, copies of the petition were lodged in every market town in Northamptonshire for local people to sign.

The returned petition sheets were reported to contain over 1800 names from across the county: farmers, tradesmen, professionals, and townsfolk who believed the trade in human beings had to end.

A few years later, in 1792, the Northamptonshire Baptist Association added its formal support. At its annual meeting, the Association voted five guineas for the Committee for the Abolition of the Slave Trade in London; modest in monetary terms, but symbolically important as a public commitment from a countywide network of chapels whose members were already signing and circulating petitions.

A second wave of Northamptonshire petitions came in the 1830s, when the focus had shifted from ending the trade to abolishing slavery itself within the British Empire.

On 9 November 1830, in the House of Lords, Earl Spencer again appeared as the carrier of local opinion. He presented petitions from Northampton town, and from five other parishes across the county.

Taken together, these episodes show that Northamptonshire was not a silent spectator of the national abolition movement. From the meetings at the George Inn and the Town Hall in 1788, to chapel resolutions and later parish petitions carried into the Lords in 1830, people across the county repeatedly used the only direct political instrument most of them possessed, their signatures, to demand an end to a system they had come to see as cruel, unjust, and unworthy of a "great and free" nation.

Nonconformist Northamptonshire

Northamptonshire was unusually fertile ground for the growth of abolitionist ideas, and a big reason for this lay deep in its religious culture. Throughout the eighteenth and early nineteenth centuries, the county was home to a dense network of Nonconformist congregations (Baptists, Independents, and Quakers) whose beliefs and practices placed them outside the authority of the Church of England.

These communities nurtured a spirit of independence, moral seriousness, and social reform that proved crucial to the abolition movement.

Nonconformist chapels operated beyond the control of elite landowning families and political patrons; they were independent from the Catholic Church and the Church of England. Their ministers were often chosen by the congregation, not appointed by bishops or aristocrats, and were therefore freer to speak boldly on national issues.

Many Nonconformist ministers preached that slave-trading was a national sin; that all people were equal before God; and that Christians had a duty to oppose injustice wherever they found it. In these spaces, moral arguments could flourish without fear of offending powerful local interests.

The Baptist churches of Kettering, Olney, and Roade; the Independent congregations at Castle Hill and elsewhere; and the Quaker meetings at Northampton, Wellingborough, and Finedon all contributed to a culture that took conscience seriously.

Northampton's Nonconformist communities, supported by networks of correspondence, visiting preachers, and shared theological commitments, became part of the national infrastructure that helped turn public opinion against slavery.

This Nonconformist landscape did not abolish the slave trade on its own, but it shaped the minds of those who would. It helped create the environment in which figures like Andrew Fuller, John Sutcliff, William Carey, and later William Knibb formed their convictions, sharpened their conscience, and carried Northamptonshire's voice into the wider world.

The Northamptonshire Baptist Movement and Abolition

The Baptist communities of Northamptonshire played an important role in shaping the county's contribution to the national abolition movement. Their influence did not rest solely on a handful of remarkable individuals, but on a wider culture of dissent, cooperation, and moral seriousness that characterised the Northamptonshire Baptist Association during the late eighteenth and early nineteenth centuries.

The Northamptonshire Baptist Association, founded in the early eighteenth century, provided the organisational backbone for these views. Churches met annually to share news, support one another, resolve disputes, and consider matters of theology and practice.

Through these meetings, ideas travelled quickly from congregation to congregation. A sermon preached in Olney could influence thinking in Kettering; a concern raised in Roade could become a topic for discussion across the Midlands. This network enabled the county's Baptists to function as a cohesive movement, united by shared convictions and a common sense of spiritual responsibility.

Within this framework, a distinctive culture of conscience emerged. Northamptonshire Baptists placed great importance on moral reform, both personal and national. They frequently spoke of "national sins," believing that societies, not only individuals, could stand under divine judgement for wrongdoing.

This outlook made the horrors of the slave trade not merely a political issue, but a *spiritual* one. Baptists understood slavery as an affront to God's creation and a stain on the nation's character. Such ideas were rooted in their theology, which emphasised the equal worth of all people and the duty of Christians to oppose injustice wherever it was found.

News of suffering, brutality, and resistance among enslaved communities, especially in the West Indies, sharpened the sense that Christians had a responsibility not only to preach the gospel, but to stand against such oppression.

This movement-wide environment helps explain why Northamptonshire produced such a notable cluster of abolition-minded figures.

When petitions against the slave trade were issued, Baptist congregations signed them. When sermons were preached condemning the trade, chapels were full. When sugar boycotts spread, Baptist families often participated. These actions were not isolated gestures but expressions of a shared conviction that the slave trade was incompatible with Christian faith and human dignity.

By the 1830s, as missionary letters from Jamaica and other colonies revealed the harsh realities of slavery more vividly, Northamptonshire's Baptist communities became part of a national groundswell of public pressure. Their chapels echoed the arguments heard in Parliament and reinforced them in local consciousness. In this way, the Baptist movement in Northamptonshire contributed to the moral climate that made abolition possible.

The story of abolition in Northamptonshire, therefore, is not only about the politicians who became national figures or the missionaries who witnessed injustice firsthand. It is also about the congregations, ordinary men, women, and families, who created a culture in which the arguments for abolition could take root, grow, and flourish.

Voter Reform Bills

Lord Althorp, Member of Parliament for Northamptonshire, was a key figure in steering the Reform Act of 1832 through Parliament.

In the early 1800s, Britain's voting system was dominated by wealthy landowners and owners of overseas plantations. Many of them controlled tiny "rotten boroughs" which had hardly any voters, but they still sent MPs to Parliament. This meant the enslavers had a built-in political advantage and could block attempts to end slavery simply by keeping their supporters in these safe seats.

The Reform Act of 1832 weakened this power. It abolished rotten boroughs and gave seats to growing towns and cities, where large numbers of middle-class people, Nonconformists, evangelicals, and supporters of social reform now had a political voice.

These new voters were far more likely to back abolition, and MPs could no longer ignore the petitions and pressure coming from their expanded constituencies.

By reducing the planters' influence and strengthening the voices of ordinary citizens, voter reform made it much harder for Parliament to protect slavery. This shift helped create the political conditions needed for the Slavery Abolition Act of 1833.

In short, changing who had power in elections changed what Parliament was able to do.

PART III

Northamptonshire's Key Figures

Sir William Dolben

Sir William Dolben was a Northamptonshire MP who became one of the earliest politicians to challenge the cruelty of the slave trade.

His personal turning point came when he visited a slave ship docked in London and was horrified by what he saw: hundreds of people crammed together in terrible conditions for the long voyage across the Atlantic.

Dolben decided that Parliament had to act.

In 1788 he introduced a new law, later known as Dolben's Act, which placed strict limits on how many enslaved people could be packed onto a British slave ship.

This was a huge moment. It proved that MPs could challenge powerful interests, and it pushed the issue of slavery to the centre of national politics.

Before 1788, Parliament regulated slavery as a business problem. Dolben's Act was the first time it regulated it as a moral one. It didn't end the slave trade, but it was the first time Parliament had ever passed a law to control it.

Dolben's actions helped set the stage for later abolitionists, who would go on to fight for the complete end of the trade and, eventually, the end of slavery itself.

He shows that sometimes big changes begin with someone simply being brave enough to say, "This is wrong, and we must do something about it."

John Charles Spencer

In the early 1830s, John Charles Spencer (Lord Althorp) was Leader of the House of Commons. This meant he helped organise debates, guide new laws, and made sure Parliament actually got things done.

By 1833, many people across Britain had been demanding an end to slavery for *years*, but turning that into a real law was still extremely difficult. That's where Spencer made the difference. He helped steer the Slavery Abolition Act through Parliament.

The Slavery Abolition Act itself was a mixture of victory and compromise. Young enslaved children were freed straight away, but most adults had to work as "apprentices" for several more years before gaining full freedom.

Even so, the 1833 law marked a huge turning point. It showed that the government was finally prepared to change the system, and it led directly to the end of slavery in Britain's colonies.

The Slavery Abolition Act might not have gotten through if not for one of Spencer's other achievements. He was also responsible for enacting Voter Reform, giving a voice to abolition-minded people.

Philip Doddridge

Philip Doddridge (1702–1751) was a celebrated Northampton minister, educator, and hymn-writer. He provided one of the earliest and most enduring moral frameworks that would later nourish abolitionist thought.

As head of the Northampton Academy, Doddridge trained ministers who carried his values of conscience, compassion, and spiritual equality across Britain and the Atlantic world.

Doddridge's legacy did not end at Northampton. His written works, particularly his book *The Rise and Progress of Religion in the Soul* helped his influence spread.

One of the most important inheritors of that influence was a young man who had once been adrift at sea and spiritually unanchored: John Newton.

John Newton

John Newton (1725–1807), author of hymn *Amazing Grace*, was a pastor whose ministry was at Olney, just beyond the Northamptonshire border in Buckinghamshire.

Phillip Doddridge's book *The Rise and Progress of Religion in the Soul* had a profound spiritual influence on Newton, and while they never met in person, they exchanged letters throughout their lives.

Newton's past gave him some uncomfortable insight into the slave trade. Having worked about slave ships in his youth, he even had a brief interlude where *he himself* had been enslaved.

He went on to renounce the trade entirely, and wrote a book called *Thoughts Upon the African Slave Trade.* This served as both a personal confession and a powerful call for societal change.

Newton would later take a rectory in London, where his position as a well-known evangelical clergyman and someone who was publicly repentant about his past in the slave trade led him to become the spiritual mentor of the man who would lead the parliamentary fight against the slave trade: William Wilberforce.

William Wilberforce

William Wilberforce (1759–1833) was not a Northamptonshire figure himself, but the county shaped the turning point of his life.

In 1785, uncertain whether to leave politics for religion, he sought the counsel of John Newton. Newton, drawing on the moral tradition that linked back to Doddridge, urged him to remain in Parliament *and* serve as a Christian in public life.

Wilberforce later said this meeting "reclaimed" him, and soon he set his sights on his "Great Object", that of ending the slave trade. Newton supported him throughout the long campaign, offering both testimony and pastoral strength.

Andrew Fuller

Andrew Fuller (1754–1815), minister of a Baptist church in Kettering, became one of the most influential voices in the evangelical world of the late eighteenth century.

Best known for shaping the theology of the Baptist Missionary Society, Fuller was also a committed opponent of the slave trade.

He was part of a generation of Baptists who believed that national sins must be confronted openly. When Christians across the country debated the slave trade, Fuller's voice consistently came down on the side of its condemnation.

In Kettering, he helped cultivate an environment that valued moral reform, humanitarian concern, and global awareness. These ideas shaped the young ministers around him, including the missionary reformer who began his journey just a few miles away: William Carey.

William Carey

William Carey (1761–1834) was born in Paulerspury on the edge of Northamptonshire. As a young cobbler, he grew up in an environment where the values of equality, conscience, and reform were preached from chapel pulpits. These ideas would stay with him for life.

Before becoming the "father of modern missions", Carey was known for his strong moral convictions; local accounts recall that he refused to buy sugar, a small but significant act of protest against the slave-produced commodity that dominated British kitchens.

His prayers frequently included the enslaved, and he wrote and spoke passionately about human equality long before starting his missionary work.

Carey was part of the Northamptonshire Baptist Association, where he worked alongside Andrew Fuller and John Sutcliff. Their partnership would give birth to the Baptist Missionary Society in 1792. They helped cultivate an intellectual and spiritual climate in which slavery was increasingly seen as incompatible with Christian faith.

Carey's outward-looking vision was shared by his close friend at Olney, whose chapel became a centre of abolitionist conviction: John Sutcliff.

John Sutcliff

John Sutcliff (1752–1814), pastor of the Baptist church in Olney, stands as one of the most important but least recognised abolitionist voices in the Midlands.

A close friend of both Andrew Fuller and William Carey, Sutcliff was a central figure in the Northamptonshire Baptist Association, where he drove much of the early moral and organisational energy that defined the movement.

Sutcliff believed passionately that Christians must speak out against injustice. Under Sutcliff's leadership, member churches contributed funds to the London abolition committee, the same group that supported Wilberforce's early Parliamentary efforts.

His Olney chapel, standing only a few miles from where John Newton had once preached, became a hub of evangelical activism.

Sutcliff rallied ministers to think globally, pray earnestly, and act responsibly. In doing so, he helped establish a moral culture that would influence not only the Midlands but also some of the most dramatic abolitionist campaigns abroad; none more so than those led by the next figure shaped by the Northamptonshire tradition: William Knibb.

William Knibb

William Knibb (1803–1845) was born in Kettering, raised in a Nonconformist community that inherited the legacy of Fuller, Carey, and Sutcliff. He also attended a Sunday School which was established by Reverend Thomas Northcote Toller.

Knibb travelled to Jamaica as a missionary in the 1820s and quickly became an outspoken defender of the island's enslaved population.

His fearless preaching, his refusal to accept racial hierarchy, and his willingness to challenge plantation authorities made him a target for hostility.

During the unrest of the early 1830s, Knibb was arrested and briefly imprisoned for defending enslaved people's rights, a scandal that reverberated back to Britain.

On returning home, Knibb embarked on a powerful speaking tour across the country. His speeches electrified audiences. He testified before Parliamentary committees, provided first-hand accounts of violence and oppression, and urged MPs to act decisively.

Thomas Toller

Following in the footsteps of his father (Thomas *Northcote* Toller), Reverend Thomas Toller was part of a ministerial dynasty that led the same church for over a century.

His ministry was rooted in social reform, education, and moral responsibility.

In 1832, Toller helped to found **the Kettering Anti-Slavery Auxiliary Association**, working with prominent townsmen such as John Cooper Gotch and his son Thomas Henry Gotch [5]. Their united voices were among those calling for abolition.

Toller was also among those calling for the Reform Acts, which would change who could vote, shifting the power away from those who had an interest in maintaining slavery.

The Montagus

The Montagu family are often remembered for their unusually humane treatment of Ignatius Sancho. He credited the 2nd Duke and Duchess with providing him education, stability, and opportunities rare for a black child in eighteenth-century Britain.

A well-known family portrait from Boughton House includes a young black page, known as "Charles the Black", depicted with a dignity uncommon in aristocratic imagery of the period.

In this portrait, Charles appears wearing a metal collar, a feature not uncommon in aristocratic art of the period, likely intended as decorative livery rather than a literal shackle. These depictions often exoticised black attendants, reflecting artistic conventions rather than personal beliefs.

Although the portrait reflects the hierarchical imagery of its age, household ledgers show that Charles was earning a wage, and he must have been well thought of to be included in such a portrait.

While these examples suggest a measure of benevolence within the household, there is no evidence that the Montagus were active supporters of the abolition movement.

PART IV

Black Lives in Northamptonshire

Although the transatlantic slave trade operated thousands of miles away, its human impact reached into English counties, including Northamptonshire.

The surviving evidence is fragmentary, but several individuals stand out as clear reminders that black lives, shaped by slavery and empire, formed part of the county's history. Their stories show how the global system of enslavement touched even the quietest corners of rural England.

James Chappell

James Chappell (c.1648–1730) is among the earliest documented black residents of Northamptonshire [4]. He worked at Kirby Hall, near Gretton.

A parish entry describes him as "a Negro boy aged 15, servant to Lord Christopher Hatton", added at a time when black servants were rare but not unknown in aristocratic households.

Chappell remained in the Hatton household for many years, and even saved the lives of family members following a gunpowder explosion.

He was left a pension of more than £20 every year for the rest of his life by Lord Hatton, a huge sum in those days.

Local tradition holds that he went on to run the Hatton Arms in Gretton, suggesting a degree of independence unusual for black servants in seventeenth century England.

His surviving record is only a handful of lines in a parish book, but James Chappell stands as one of the county's earliest known black inhabitants, and a reminder that black lives were present in Northamptonshire long before the abolition movement began.

Caesar Shaw

Another Northamptonshire-linked figure is Caesar Shaw [H]. Historic England identifies him as having been owned by John Spencer of Althorp and baptised in Northampton, placing him firmly within the county's social landscape.

Shaw's presence illustrates how baptism did not necessarily mean freedom; many enslaved individuals in Britain were baptised at the insistence of their masters while remaining bound by legal and economic control.

Little more is known about his life, but that single entry, an enslaved African man brought into one of Northamptonshire's most prominent households, is powerful evidence of how the structures of slavery reached into the English countryside.

Anthony Williams

Perhaps the most moving evidence of all is found in a churchyard at Blatherwycke, and the inscription on the gravestone of Anthony Williams [7].

IN MEMORY OF
ANTHONY WILLIAMS
WHO WAS DROWNED
IN BLATHERWYCKE LAKE
JUNE 11 1836
AGED 29 YEARS

-

HERE A POOR WANDERER HATH FOUND A GRAVE
WHO DEATH EMBRACED WHILST STRUGGLING WITH THE WAVE
HIS HOME FAR OFF IN THE BROAD INDIAN MAIN
HE LEFT TO RID HIMSELF OF SLAVERYS CHAIN.
FRIENDLESS AND COMFORTLESS HE PASSED THE SEA
ON ALBION'S SHORES TO SEEK FOR LIBERTY
YET VAIN HIS SEARCH FOR AYE WITH TOILING BROW
HE NEVER FOUND HIS FREEDOM UNTIL NOW

While contemporary sources agree that he *did* drown, later elaborations (likely false) state that he drowned saving the life of his master.

The poem on his grave is one of the few surviving memorials in the county that directly confronts the reality of enslavement, making him a crucial figure in Northamptonshire's abolition landscape.

Ignatius Sancho

Ignatius Sancho (c.1729–1780) was a writer, shopkeeper, and the first known black Briton to vote. He spent part of his early life serving the Montagu family, whose country seat was Boughton House, near Kettering.

Born on a slave ship and later brought to England as a young child, he was enslaved or a semi-enslaved servant before the Montagus intervened. Under their patronage he received education, stability, and access to London's intellectual life.

But Sancho's most historically significant achievement came later, when he became the first known black person to vote in a British parliamentary election.

At a time when voting rights depended entirely on property, Sancho did something unusual for a black man in eighteenth-century Britain: he established his own business.

After getting married, he opened a small grocery shop in Westminster. As the legal "householder" responsible for paying taxes, Sancho met the precise qualifications required to vote in borough elections.

Why these stories matter

James Chappell, Caesar Shaw, Anthony Williams, Ignatius Sancho, and the wider circle connected to estates like Boughton House reveal a crucial truth: slavery was not a distant phenomenon. Its victims and survivors lived in English homes, walked the streets of Northamptonshire villages, worked in local households, and found their final resting place in the county's soil.

Their experiences stand alongside the petitions, sermons, meetings, and campaigns that would later make Northamptonshire a strong voice for abolition. Together they form a fuller picture of the county's history, one in which both the injustice of slavery and the determination to end it played out in local lives.

Northamptonshire's records include rare mentions of non-European individuals long before the transatlantic slave trade, such as Peter the Saracen in the medieval period. But these earlier figures belonged to a completely different historical world and context, and are not connected to the later history of slavery or abolition.

PART V

The Aftermath: The 1833 Abolition Act and the Apprenticeship System

When the Slavery Abolition Act received Royal Assent in 1833, many people across Northamptonshire believed the long struggle against slavery had finally succeeded.

The news reached chapels, newspapers, market squares, and meeting houses, and the county responded with a mixture of relief, pride, and heartfelt thanksgiving.

Celebrations and Thanksgiving Services

Several churches in Northampton marked the moment with special services of thanksgiving. Congregations gathered to hear sermons giving thanks for what they understood as the end of slavery throughout the British Empire.

Hymns were sung, prayers offered, and ministers spoke of the victory of Christian conscience over a national sin that had burdened Britain for generations.

For many in Northamptonshire, far removed from Britain's ports and plantations, it felt like the moral conclusion of the abolition story. A great injustice had been named, opposed, and finally overturned.

The Problem of "Apprenticeship"

The reality in the Caribbean was far more complex. Although slavery had been abolished in law, most formerly enslaved adults were forced into a compulsory period of unpaid labour under a scheme known as "apprenticeship", intended to last until 1840.

It was promoted in Britain as a gentle transition to freedom, but on the ground it operated much like the old system: restrictive, coercive, and deeply resented by the people living under it.

In Northamptonshire, news of this system arrived unevenly. For the majority of residents, the celebrations overshadowed the troubling details of apprenticeship.

Local records show little organised campaigning against the scheme. Having fought hard during the earlier anti-slavery years, many in the county believed their part was done.

But not everyone was silent.

Voices Raised Against the System

The strongest denunciations heard in Northamptonshire came from someone the county knew well: William Knibb, the Kettering-born Baptist missionary whose work in Jamaica made him a national figure.

Returning to Britain during the 1830s, Knibb visited Northamptonshire and spoke at meetings in places such as College Street Chapel, describing firsthand the abuses of "Apprenticeship", and insisting that true freedom had not yet arrived in the Caribbean.

His speeches helped many in the county understand that slavery had ended in name, not in practice. Some congregations joined the national call for apprenticeship to be terminated early, adding their voices to the moral pressure building across Britain.

Though surviving evidence suggests no resulting major local petitioning movement, Northamptonshire's Nonconformist communities were receptive to Knibb's testimony and supported the wider abolitionist cause as it entered its final phase.

Freedom Achieved

Under mounting pressure from campaigners across Britain, including Knibb, whose powerful testimony shook Parliament, the apprenticeship system was abolished ahead of schedule on 1 August 1838.

It was that day when Knibb declared to a vast congregation in Jamaica:

"The monster is dead."

And with those words, the long, uneven progress from abolition to freedom reached its true conclusion.

For Northamptonshire, the aftermath of 1833 was a mixture of celebration, and renewed, if uneven, commitment to justice.

The county that had contributed so much to the earlier phases of abolition now stood witness to the final end of slavery in the British Empire.

Thank you for reading!

If you enjoyed this book, please consider leaving a review.

It really helps writers and helps other readers find the book too.

Sources

[1]
The Baptist Reporter (1846) *William Knibb, The Negro Liberator.*
https://missiology.gospelstudies.org.uk/pdf/baptist-reporter/baptist-recorder-ns_1846_076.pdf

[2]
Northamptonshire Archives (2013) *Boots and shoes in Northamptonshire.*
https://www.northamptonshirebootandshoe.org.uk/wp-content/uploads/2013/07/Boot-and-Shoe-Industry.pdf

[3]
Berg, M. and Hudson, P. (2021) "Slavery, Atlantic trade and skills: a response to Mokyr's 'Holy Land of Industrialism", *Journal of the British Academy*, Vol 9, pp. 259-281
https://www.thebritishacademy.ac.uk/documents/3549/JBA-9-p259-Berg-Hudson.pdf

[4]
Northamptonshire Heritage (2020) *Slavery and the abolition of slavery.*
https://www.northamptonshireheritage.co.uk/learn/historical-events-and-movements/Pages/slavery.html

[5]
Northampton Mercury (1788) *26 January*

> There is no Doubt but that many other respectable Characters would have attended the Meeting for the Suppression of the Slave Trade, had there been one publicly called. But, besides the Trouble it must have occasioned to distant Parts of the County, on a Matter, concerning which there could scarcely be two Opinions, the Business is expected to come on so very soon after the Meeting of Parliament that Time would not permit it. The Subject pressed for an immediate Decision; it being proper that the Petition should reach the House, before the Matter is brought into Discussion.
>
> As, on Account of the early Meeting of Parliament, only about a Week longer can be allowed before the Copies of the Petition for the Suppression of the SLAVE TRADE, left in the Market Towns, are to be returned, in order that the said Petition may be presented to the House of Commons; it is earnestly to be wished that the Gentlemen and the Clergy of the County would kindly interest themselves to promote the Signing thereof as soon as possible among the Freeholders and others of their respective Parishes. An Application to Parliament, which has so benevolent an Object in View, should not want the Force which Numbers, as well as Respectability, can give it.
>
> It is hoped that the Inhabitants of the County of every Denomination (for the Matter is not confined to the *Freeholders* only) will shew their Humanity and Benevolence by signing the Petition, left in different Parts, for the Suppression of the Slave Trade. A Traffic, replete with every Species of Oppression and Cruelty towards an inoffensive Race of Men, and which violates all the Laws that Religion and Justice prescribe for the Treatment of our Fellow-Creatures.

[6]
Buckell, J. (2022) "Slavery and Anti-slavery in Northamptonshire", *Northamptonshire Past and Present*, No 75, pp 38-55
Available at:
https://www.northamptonshirerecordsociety.org.uk/pdf/npp/number/npp-n75.pdf

[7]
Wilson, J. (2020) *Peeling off the legends – the grave of a former slave who became a valued estate servant*
https://churchmonumentssociety.org/monument-of-the-month/the-monument-to-anthony-williams-d-1836-at-blatherwycke-northamptonshire